PELICANS

Tim Harris

Grolier
an imprint of

www.scholastic.com/librarypublishing

Published 2008 by Grolier
An imprint of Scholastic Library Publishing
Old Sherman Turnpike, Danbury,
Connecticut 06816

For The Brown Reference Group plc
Project Editor: Jolyon Goddard
Copy-editors: Lesley Ellis, Lisa Hughes,
    Wendy Horobin
Picture Researcher: Clare Newman
Designers: Jeni Child, Lynne Ross,
    Sarah Williams
Managing Editor: Bridget Giles

Volume ISBN-13: 978-0-7172-6241-0
Volume ISBN-10: 0-7172-6241-3

**Library of Congress
Cataloging-in-Publication Data**

Nature's children. Set 1.
    p. cm.
    Includes index.
    ISBN-13: 978-0-7172-8080-3
    ISBN-10: 0-7172-8080-2
    1. Animals--Encyclopedias, Juvenile.
    QL49.N38 2007
    590--dc22

                    2007018358

Printed and bound in China

PICTURE CREDITS

Front Cover: Nature PL: Lynn M. Stone.

Back Cover: NHPA: James Carmichael Jr.;
Shutterstock: Chuch Aghoian, David Rollins,
Kristian Sekulic.

Alamy: John White Photos 21; **Corbis**:
Dan Guravich 5, 33, 37, Martin Harvey 29;
FLPA: Tui De Roy/Minden Pictures 34,
Suzi Eszterhas/Minden Pictures 30; **NHPA**:
Rich Kirchner 42; **Photolibrary.com**:
Phyllis Greenberg 10; **Shutterstock**: Ivan
Cholakov 9, Laurin Rinder 4, 13, Ian Walker
6, Brad Whitsitt 26–27, Zimmytws 17; **Still
Pictures**: Michel and Christine Denis-Huot
2–3, 14, Freelens Pool/Animal-aff 18, 41, Ron
Giling 46, Casiano Luis/BIOS 45, Gunther
Michel/BIOS 38, M. Woike 22.

Contents

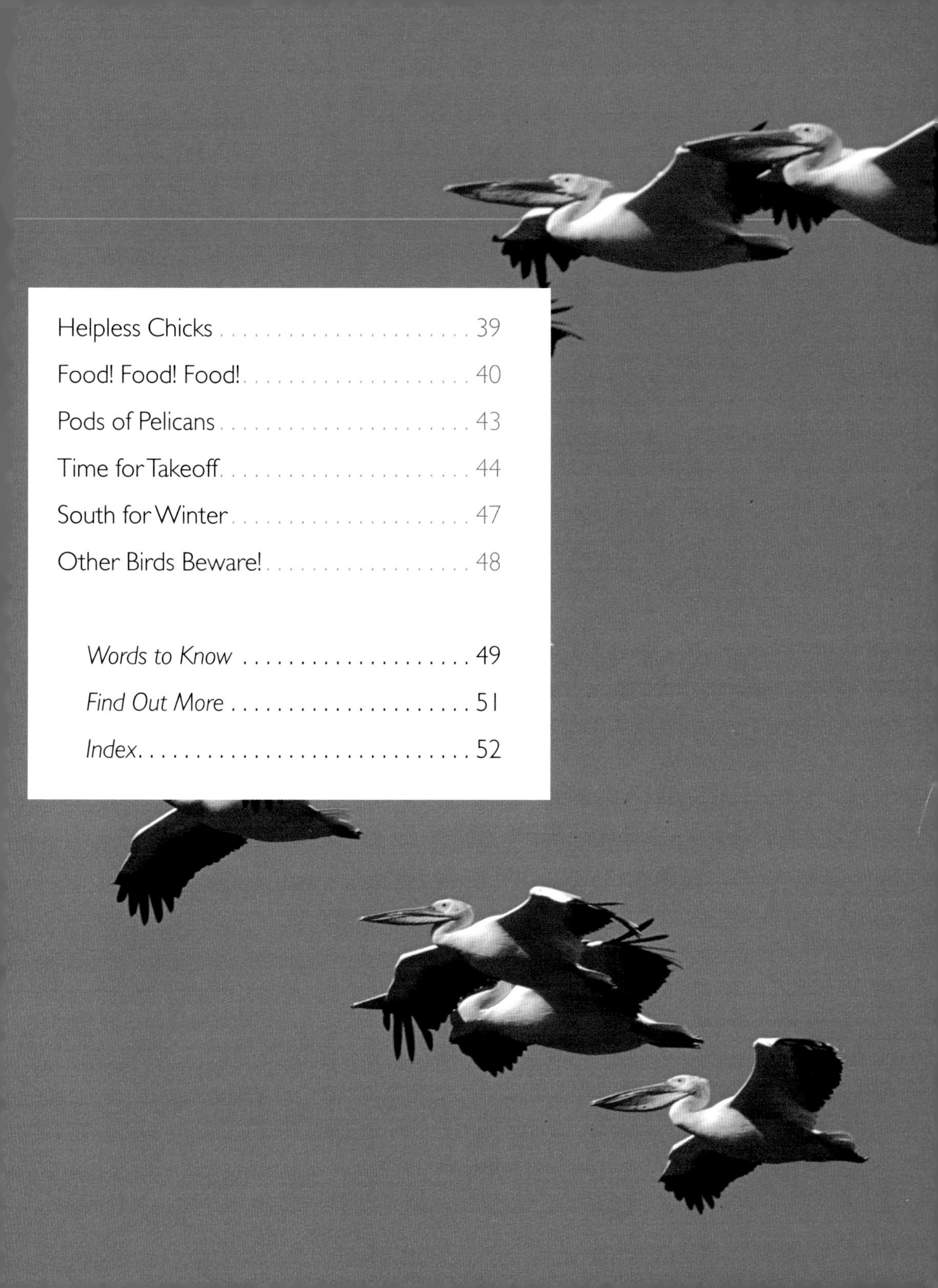

FACT FILE: Pelicans

Class	Birds (Aves)
Order	Pelican-like birds (Pelecaniformes)
Family	Pelican family (Pelecanidae)
Genus	*Pelecanus*
Species	Eight species worldwide. In North America, there are two species: American white pelican (*Pelecanus erythrorhynchos*) and brown pelican (*Pelecanus occidentalis*)
World distribution	North and South America; other species live in most parts of the world, except Antarctica
Habitat	Lakes, rivers, and seashore
Distinctive physical characteristics	Long pointed beak, with a large throat pouch on the underside; wide wingspan
Habits	Nest in colonies; build nests on the ground; travel in flocks, often in a "V" formation
Diet	Mostly fish

Introduction

Pelicans are odd-looking birds. They have **webbed feet** and a long beak with a **pouch** beneath. Pelicans also have short legs and a big body. Even though they look clumsy, pelicans are good fliers and excellent swimmers. They are closely related to cormorants, boobies, gannets, and frigate birds.

Pelicans live along ocean coastlines and around inland lakes in most warm regions of the world. Some pelicans fly long distances to avoid winter.

A pelican in its nest keeps its eggs warm by sitting on them.

A brown pelican's huge beak is ideal for catching fish.

Big Beaks

The first thing you notice about a pelican is its beak. The beak can grow to 2 feet (60 cm) long—about the length of your arm! Having such a huge beak helps the pelican catch lots of fish. A pelican can hold more food in its beak than any other type of bird.

These strange-looking birds are among the largest birds in North America. Adult American white pelicans sometimes weigh more than 22 pounds (10 kg). That is as heavy as a one-year-old baby! A pelican's long, broad wings and powerful wing muscles help make the heavy bird a great flier.

The pelican's webbed feet are not much good for walking, but they are useful in water. The webs of skin between the toes of the feet help a pelican swim fast when chasing a tasty fish.

Life on the Water

There are eight different types of pelicans in the world. At least one type lives on every continent except Antarctica. Pelicans spend their whole life close to water. That's because water is home to the pelican's favorite food: fish!

There are two types of pelicans in North America: American white pelicans and brown pelicans. American white pelicans live on and around lakes, swamps, and coastal marshes. They live mostly in the western United States. Brown pelicans live on offshore islands and onshore along the coasts of the United States.

Pelicans do not stay in the same place all the time. They often fly short distances in search of fish. Some pelicans fly much longer distances to escape cold weather in winter.

The tip of a
pelican's beak is
hooked to help
the pelican hold
onto slippery fish.

9

The underside of a brown pelican's wings have silvery gray streaks.

Feathers Galore

Pelicans are mostly white in color. American white pelicans are almost pure white, except for the dark flight feathers on their wings. Wing feathers need to be very tough, and dark-colored feathers are stronger than white feathers. They are stronger because the pigment that provides color helps strengthen the protein (an organic material) that feathers are made from.

As its name suggests, the brown pelican is mostly covered with brown feathers, but it has silvery gray streaks and white markings on the underside of its wings.

Feathers are tough, but they do not last forever. Pelicans, like other birds, replace their feathers with new ones every year. This process is called **molting**. While a pelican molts its flight feathers, it cannot fly.

Powerful Fliers

Pelicans are powerful fliers. But because they are heavy birds, they have to work hard to take off. They build up speed by running across water, beating their wings, and pumping their feet as fast as they can. When pelicans are traveling fast enough, they rise into the air. Once airborne, pelicans fly with their head pulled back and their beak pouch resting lightly on their chest.

What makes pelicans such strong fliers? They have huge wings! Take three long strides across the floor: that is the length of an American white pelican's wings when they are stretched out! One stride measures the width of the wings. Pelicans' large wings and powerful flight muscles let them fly for hours without needing a break. On long journeys they can fly very high— sometimes more than 9,000 feet (3,000 m).

A brown pelican
in flight.

A flock of American white pelicans flies in a "V" formation.

14

Flying in Flocks

Pelicans are very social birds. They do almost everything together—and that includes flying. Sometimes dozens might fly in a flock in search of a better area to fish. When they are flying long distances, or **migrating**, hundreds of pelicans travel together. Often, they travel one behind the other in a long line. At other times they fly in a wide "V" pattern.

Pelicans do not need to beat their wings quickly to stay in the air. They flap slowly, with frequent glides: flap, flap, flap, and glide. If they find a column of rising air, called a **thermal**, pelicans do not have to flap at all. Instead they glide on the thermal, circling around and around, higher and higher. They are certainly graceful fliers. But there is nothing graceful about a pelican landing. They often plop down on the water making a huge splash, with their feet stuck out in front, acting as brakes.

Going Fishing

Pelicans are expert fishers. Their beak and pouch are their special tools for catching fish. Together, these serve as a large dip net. The pelican dips its beak into the water and scoops up a pouchful of water. If the bird is lucky, it will scoop up some fish, too. Then the pelican simply squeezes out the water and swallows the fish whole. If a fish tries to escape from the pouch, the hooked tip of the pelican's beak helps the bird snatch it back.

The pouch is stretchy. It can hold just under 10 quarts (9.5 l) of water. To see for yourself how much that is, fill a one-quart (1 l) carton with water and empty it into the sink. Do that 10 times, and you'll see just how much water a pelican's pouch can hold.

A pelican opens
its beak underwater
and scoops up
a tasty fish.

A brown pelican tips its head back to swallow the fish in its pouch.

18

A Handy Pouch

The pouch is very useful for catching fish, but a pelican does not keep the food in its pouch for long. Once the pelican squeezes the water out, the bird simply tips its head back, and the fish slides down its throat.

A pelican's throat and stomach are expandable, too. When fishing is good, the birds stuff themselves to the brim. They may eat several hundred small fish, totaling about 8 pounds (3.5 kg), in next to no time. Sometimes, pelicans eat so much they cannot take off to fly!

When pelicans are feeding their chicks, the parents mash up a fishy meal in their stomach, and then cough it back up, or **regurgitate** it, into the pouch. The young birds then feed from the parent's pouch. The pouch has another use: cooling the pelican. When the bird is very hot, it flutters the moist skin of its pouch. Air then moves around the bird, cooling it. Dogs do a similar thing when they stick out their tongue and pant very quickly.

Paddle Power

A pelican has four forward-pointing toes on each foot. Like the feet of many other birds that spend most of their time in water, webs of skin connect each of these toes. Webbed feet help the pelican swim, much like flippers help a diver. As the pelican pushes its feet backward in the water, the bird moves forward quickly.

Webbed feet are good for swimming. But they are a bit of a nuisance when the birds are walking. Pelicans move awkwardly on land and have to waddle, or throw their body from side to side, to move along. Fortunately, pelicans do not have to walk very much. They mostly get around by swimming or flying.

Pelicans' webbed feet are clumsy for walking, but they're excellent paddles for swimming.

American white
pelicans team
up to improve
their chances
of catching fish.

Teamwork

All pelicans eat fish, but they do not all catch their fish in the same way. American white pelicans dip their beak, and sometimes their head, underwater as they swim. They open their beak and scoop up their food. Common prey includes fish such as minnows, perch, suckers, and carp. Sometimes the pelicans catch and eat frogs and salamanders, too.

Pelicans may fish alone in deep water, but in shallow water they often work together. When a school of fish swims among them, the birds quickly form a ring around it. They then herd the fish toward the center. When the fish are trapped in the middle, the pelicans feed in a wild frenzy of jabbing beaks and splashing feet. Each bird gets a bigger meal than it would have by fishing on its own.

Dive-bombers

What was that big splash out in the water? It was probably a pelican diving for a fish. Usually, the pelicans plunge from a height of about 23 feet (7 m). When they see a school of fish, they pick their target and ...whoosh!... they splash into the water. The pelican can twist its body to change the direction of its dive if the fish move unexpectedly. Dive-bombing brown pelicans make a huge splash when they hit the water. Brown pelicans catch small fish that live in schools, such as pigfish, pinfish, sheepshead, and silversides.

Why don't the pelicans hurt themselves when they hit the water? There is air trapped among their feathers and in pockets under their skin. That cushions and protects the birds from the impact of the water.

Communication

Pelicans are not noisy birds. In fact, away from their nests they are usually silent. In their breeding colonies, adult American white pelicans communicate with each other by making quiet, low grunting or croaking sounds. Young birds make a weak, sneezy bark. Young brown pelicans make groaning or screeching calls. These sounds must mean something to the birds, but people do not know the exact meaning of these sounds.

Pelicans can also communicate with each other without making a sound. When two American white pelicans meet each other, they sometimes puff out their pouches, point their beaks straight up, and turn their heads slowly from side to side. Scientists think that is their way of saying, "Hi there!"

Three brown pelicans
dive for fish.

Time to Court

Pelicans are ready to raise their own families at the age of three or four years. American white pelicans **mate** in spring. Brown pelicans mate at any time of the year, depending on where they live.

Before they can mate, pelicans must choose a partner. That is called pairing. Male pelicans try to attract a partner by showing off. How do they show off? They perform **courtship** dances, which might involve slowly walking around a female, stamping their flat feet as they go. Or the male may bow his head and beak to the female, as if to say, "Choose me! I'm the best!"

A male and a female white pelican size each other up.

When the brown pelican's
head feathers turn yellow,
it is ready to mate.

Looking Good!

Pelicans make themselves brighter and more attractive before they start courting. For most of the year the pouch under the beak of an American white pelican is dull. But in February, it turns bright orange and remains that way throughout the breeding season. At the same time, the birds grow a furry orange bump on their beak. Little patches of skin around pelicans' eyes also become brighter during the breeding season.

Brown pelicans change even more dramatically when they are ready to mate. They replace their white neck feathers with brown feathers, and the feathers on their head become bright yellow. These changes help the birds draw attention to themselves.

Pelican Colonies

Pelicans are social birds. They prefer to feed and fly with other pelicans. They also prefer to build their nests, lay their eggs, and raise their chicks together, too. Sometimes a big pelican city, or **colony**, contains several hundred nests. Because pelicans eat fish and feed their young on fish, they form their colonies near water.

American white pelicans nest on islands in lakes. Brown pelicans mostly build their nests on offshore islands. By nesting on islands, they keep many land-living **predators**—such as rats and foxes—from eating their eggs and chicks. Pelicans are easily scared away from their nests. Sometimes, if people get too close to a nest the parents will fly away and not return. When that happens, the eggs go cold and will not **hatch**. Abandoned chicks will starve to death.

Brown pelicans are social
birds. This group lives
on North Island, Louisiana.

A male brown pelican carries a twig for its nest.

Building a Home

Some birds spend weeks building neat nests. Not pelicans! Their nests are very simple. A pair of brown pelicans gathers sticks and bits of wood to make a simple platform on the ground. They make sure there is a hole in the middle. After the birds have mated, the female lays two or three eggs in the hole.

An American white pelican spends even less time building its nest. This type of pelican sits on the ground and turns around and around, dragging its beak along the ground and pulling in twigs, stones, and earth to make a saucerlike ring. There, the female lays her eggs. The parents look after the eggs in the nest until the chicks hatch. Then the parents feed the chicks in the nest until they are big enough to walk. At this time, the nest is abandoned.

A colony of pelican nests is messy, crowded, and smelly! The ground is covered with their droppings, or **guano**, and rotting fish.

Egg-warmers

Mother pelicans lay two or three eggs. A group
of eggs is called a **clutch**. The adult birds must
keep the eggs warm if the tiny chicks inside are
to grow big and strong enough to hatch. That
is called **incubation**. If the eggs are left to cool,
the chicks inside will die. Most birds incubate
their eggs simply by sitting on them. Heat from
the parent's body passes through their skin and
into the eggs.

The mother and father take turns sitting
in the nest with their webbed feet covering the
eggs. Because the parents' feet are warm, the
eggs remain warm.

After about a month the eggs hatch. Now
the parents have even more work to do! They
have to keep their chicks fed until they are old
enough to care for themselves.

A pelican's big body can easily keep a clutch of eggs warm.

These newly hatched pelican chicks are helpless. They rely entirely on their parents.

Helpless Chicks

A baby pelican is completely helpless. It is a tiny pink bundle with no feathers. The chick is not the same shape as its parents, and it doesn't have a long beak. It can't fly, and it can't walk. In fact, the chick can hardly raise its head off the ground. If anything happens to the parents, the newborn will simply starve to death.

The mother and father have to help their chicks grow as fast as possible. Many times each day, the parents dribble food from the tip of their giant beak into the chicks' tiny mouth. As long as the parents can find food, the chicks will grow quickly. In the first month after the chicks hatch, they grow fluffy white feathers called **down**. These feathers are not strong enough to let the chicks fly, but the down keeps the baby birds warm.

Food! Food! Food!

Pelican chicks are always hungry! They constantly demand food from their parents. As the young pelicans grow, they learn to put their head and beak into their mother or father's pouch to grab mouthfuls of mushy, partly digested fish. This method of feeding works well. Even when the young pelican has left the nest, the adult brings it food until it can fend for itself.

Adult pelicans take good care of their young. They feed them. They also keep chicks safe from predators that may come in search of food. Attack can come from the ground or from the air. Mammals such as foxes may prowl around in search of a meal, and birds such as gulls may dive-bomb the young. Living in a colony helps all the pelicans: many pairs of eyes have a better chance of seeing an approaching predator than one pair of eyes. And even a fox is no match for a flock of adult pelicans!

A brown pelican chick reaches inside its parent's pouch for a fish dinner.

In the colony, pelican chicks gather into groups called pods.

Pods of Pelicans

Long before they are able to fly, young pelicans can walk, although not very well. They teeter and totter and often fall over, a lot like children who have just learned to walk.

Soon after becoming walkers, the young birds team up with other youngsters. They are already able to swim, so they often go to the shore in a group and spend all their time together. A group of young pelicans is called a **pod**. The pods act almost as one. If the birds are alarmed by a loud noise, they will all swim, or walk, in the same direction. Living in a pod gives the young extra protection.

The young still cannot feed themselves or fly, and their parents have to feed them several times a day. When an adult arrives, the whole pod tries to peck at the adult's beak or feet, hoping for a meal.

Time for Takeoff

Even young pelicans are heavy birds. Their feathers keep them warm but are not strong enough for flying. But by the time the chicks are about three months old, they have grown much stronger feathers in their wings. Now they are ready to fly!

Takeoffs and landings are difficult at first. The young pelicans only fly a few yards before belly-flopping on the water. Sometimes they tumble out of the air and land on one wing. But practice makes perfect, and soon they are flying confidently.

Pelicans do not get their full set of adult feathers until they are a year old. Until then, brown pelicans have a brownish gray neck and beak. Young American white pelicans have a gray back, unlike the white back of adults.

A young spot-billed
pelican tests its wings.
These pelicans live in Asia.

This brown pelican has found a warm home for winter.

South for Winter

What do pelicans do when winter is coming? They head south. Many American white pelicans raise their chicks in northern areas where winters are cold. In fall, cold winds blow and temperatures drop to near freezing. The birds leave their colonies and fly south to warmer regions, especially around the Gulf of Mexico and the Caribbean Sea.

Pelicans have large wings and powerful wing muscles. They can fly hundreds of miles in just a few weeks. By fall, the young birds are strong enough to join the adults on the long flights. The following spring, the pelicans migrate north again, returning to their colonies. There, these amazing birds with their huge beak and big webbed feet will build new nests and raise more chicks.

Other Birds Beware!

As one of the strangest-looking birds on the planet, pelicans have always attracted attention. Sometimes this has come from other birds. Seagulls and other fish-eating birds often follow pelicans to their feeding grounds in the hope of stealing fish from a pelican's pouch. Usually there is enough food to go around, but when it is scarce, pelicans must find something else to eat. Pelicans living in parks or on the coast will use their pouch to catch scraps thrown by humans. But when times are hard, pelicans have been seen eating ducklings and seagulls. The gulls are held underwater and drowned before being swallowed head first. But the hard times do not usually last long. Soon the pelicans will be feasting again on their favorite food: fish!

Words to Know

Clutch   A group of eggs.

Colony   The nesting site where hundreds of pelicans lay eggs and raise young.

Courtship   Displays, such as dancing, by adult birds to attract a mate.

Down   Very soft, fluffy feathers.

Guano   The droppings of seabirds or bats.

Hatch   To break out of an egg.

Incubation   Sitting on eggs to keep them warm so the chicks inside can grow and develop.

Mate   To come together to produce young.

Migrate   To make a long journey at regular times of the year.

49

Molt/molting	To shed one set of feathers and replace them with another set.
Pod	A group of young pelicans.
Pouch	The stretchy underside of a pelican's beak, used for catching and holding fish.
Predators	Animals that hunt other animals for food.
Regurgitate	To bring or cough up partly broken-down food. Adult pelicans bring up fish for their chicks to eat.
Thermal	A column of warm, rising air. Birds often ride on thermals to save energy.
Webbed feet	Feet with toes that are connected by flaps of skin.

Find Out More

Books

Pembrey Swan, E. *Pelicans, Cormorants, and their Kin.*
Animals in Order. London, UK: Franklin Watts,
2003.

Stone, L. M. *North American Pelicans.* Nature Watch.
Minneapolis, Minnesota: Carolrhoda Books, 2002.

Web sites

All About Birds: American White Pelican
www.birds.cornell.edu/AllAboutBirds/BirdGuide/
American_White_Pelican.html
Information about the American white pelican.

Brown Pelican
www.enchantedlearning.com/subjects/birds/printouts/
Brownpelicanprintout.shtml
Facts about the brown pelican, with a picture
to print and color in.

Index